PAREN TING

THROUGH THE STORMS *and* CHALLENGES OF LIFE

MAME YAA

ISBN 978-1-95081-824-2 (paperback)

Copyright © 2019 by Mame Yaa

All rights reserved. No part of this publication may be reproduced, distributed, or transmitted in any form or by any means, including photocopying, recording, or other electronic or mechanical methods without the prior written permission of the publisher. For permission requests, solicit the publisher via the address below.

Rushmore Press LLC
1 888 733 9607
www.rushmorepress.com

Scripture quotations marked KJV are from the Holy Bible, King James Version (Authorized Version). First published in 1611. Quoted from the KJV Classic Reference Bible, Copyright © 1983 by Zondervan Corporation.

Scripture quotations marked NIV are taken from the Holy Bible, New International Version®. Copyright © 1973, 1978, 1984 by International Bible Society. Used by permission of Zondervan. All rights reserved. [Biblica]

Printed in the United States of America

CONTENTS

Chapter 1: Introduction 5

Chapter 2: The Child's Mind 13

Chapter 3: Communication 23

Chapter 4: Values and Integrity 31

Chapter 5: Demonstration
Through Actions 39

Chapter 6: Teaching About Life's
Choices 47

Chapter 7: Your Character Brands
You Not What You Wear 59

Chapter 8: Maturation- Embracing
Our Imperfections 69

Chapter 9: The Hurt In Love/
Personality Factors 77

Chapter 10: My Home 103

Chapter 11: Our Family Desert Times....113

Chapter 12: Know Your Surroundings On The Desert.................................. 119

Chapter 13: Be Still................................. 127

Chapter 14: Surrender And Look For Possible Growth 131

Chapter 15: Trust In The Process Of Growth And Take Action....135

CHAPTER 1

INTRODUCTION

HOW DOES YOUR CHILD KNOW GOD

Most children nowadays are born to Christian-like parents who go to church or are part of a Christian service. These children are introduced to the church and all these different services or activities, e.g. singing, preaching, dancing, etc. But that is all they get. They are not shown or taught on how to let their services lead or draw them to Christ. So to them they are Christians and they are doing all they can do but what they don't know is that they have not established their relationship with Christ yet. Usually, they do these services/activities because they were told to do so or they are doing it to please the pastor, his wife, their parents, etc. in the church. Yet, some also use their services to show off; others don't even want to be disturbed to do anything. The child is not taught the meaning in doing those services, others should be blessed through it, and also their services or character should not consist of pride. These children should be taught the way to righteousness, and that God judges a man by his character. Meaning that the child will be taught the will of God. And all lessons he takes in, he will put them back out. Therefore honoring the will of God without the knowledge that he or she is doing so; that is the character the child builds. Somebody like Martha in the bible was serviceable but she forgot to use her service as way to know Jesus Christ or get closer to him. Luke 10:38-42. We show or direct these children to open the doors of their heart to Christ; but we do not teach them that when he enters their focus should only be on him and that is what Mary took or did. What if your child can sing or dance but after doing all these they do not even know who they did it for and for whose reason they are there in the first place. Also what if your child through their services have their focus on Jesus but began to look and compete with somebody else in their mind and heart thinking the other person is gaining the attention and along the line got distracted and shifted their focus from God? Children should be taught that what God has for them is only for them. They cannot compete with others to gain the attention of God. You will only gain the attention of the man who has no power of you or the universe.

Martha's services were:

- She opened her door to Jesus
- She run to prepare food for him
- She was up and about doing what activities she taught was necessary
- she was distracted with what she was doing until it became overwhelming
- She never paused to talk or listened to Christ so she could know what to do she just started doing what she taught was right- thus what man has taught her.
- She got angry and frustrated at Jesus and her sister- thinking she was pleasing man
- She started to command Jesus by telling him to do what she wanted
- Though she was rendering a service too she became bothered and worried about what her sister was not doing

All this while she had not said anything to Jesus, because she cared about the preparation or work she was doing than to ask or talk to him. Her motives were loving and pure but the priority was wrong- the meal was important than the relationship with him. And when she did she only sounded her frustration by telling Jesus to tell her sister to help with her work. To her she thought she was doing something for Jesus. And this is how we teach our kids nowadays about Christ. So they live and do things as though they are helping Christ and that they deserve a sort of reward.

But in the end Jesus straightened her path- "Martha, Martha," the Lord answered? You are worried and upset about many things, but few things are needed-or indeed only one. Mary has chosen what is better, and it will not be taken away from her.")

And what did Mary take/do? She also had a choice and she was doing her service too. But I noticed that because Jesus was there her focus was on him. I remember Jesus said - "My food is to do the will of him who sent me and to accomplish his work. John 4:34

1 Corinthians 2:14
14 The person without the Spirit does not accept the things that come from the Spirit of God but considers them foolishness, and cannot understand them because they are discerned only through the Spirit.

We need to teach our kids to be more like the apostle Paul always thanking God who always leads us in triumphal procession and through us he may spread his knowledge everywhere.

- Mary sat at the feet of the Lord and listened to what he said.
- She made her focus be on Jesus Christ
- She showed humility by sitting at his feet
- She showed patience and quietness
- She readily opened her heart to accept the word
- She enjoyed doing what she did
- She made no noise or argued with her sister
- She waited for Jesus to do the talking instead

Here, Mary offered friendship as she had also accepted him in her home and she worked to build a relationship with Lord.

We need to teach our children how to listen to God's words instead of doing too many activities without Christ.

Martha knew who to approach and make her demands- thus, this is how we teach our children about Christ. We tell them about Christ and ask them to do the rest. Thankfully, Jesus skipped her attitude and showed her the right path to take. But notice that between these two, Jesus did not call, but allowed them to make their own choices until Martha called. So we should show our children the direction to God.

CHAPTER 2

THE CHILD'S MIND

Every child when born has an empty memory and so you the parent are responsible for teaching and filling the child's memory. Whatever you fill the child's memory with becomes what he lives by. So do you notice that as the child grows whatever language you speak with the child that is the same language the child speaks back to you naturally? You take up the responsibility to teach the child how to sit, stand, walk, eat, bath, and dress up and more. The child ends up knowing how to do these things with ease because that is what is recorded in his or her memory. Therefore the child's thinking skills helps him or her to take orderly approach to solving problems.

Teaching the child to have and build their focus and concentration on Jesus allows them to know that they are never alone or without help. Their love for God deepens that it becomes hard for outside things like the love of money, fame which is a form of payment and the likes to have a place in their heart. The love of money is serious and fame which is a form of payment but not from God most high. Jesus tells us that you cannot serve God and money, Matthew 6:24. Bible said Train up a child in the way he should go: and when he is old, he will not depart from it. Proverbs 22:6.

In training up the child, we build their attitudes, knowledge, and skills so that they can apply these in their daily life and to help them establish themselves as mature individuals.

Training up these children is not just taking them to school to learn to have careers for life but it is more than that. Training up these children involves:

- Talking – you talk to them about the right paths of life when you sit at home e.g. sitting at table and everyone is relaxed. When we sit to have conversations with our family. When we hold meetings to talk about issues. When we discipline our children
- When we walk along the road or sit in our cars or are in any means of travelling, we still have to talk about the right paths with them

- When they lie down to sleep and when they get up we still have to talk to them about the right paths of life.

In doing this we have to teach them what really matters to God. So that if even they falter along the way the Godly foundation they have will make it easier to come back to the right path.

The world is so big that it provides vast roles and purposes to choose. The stuff the world provide are dangerous so if we don't teach the kids and allow them to learn from us, then they will surely learn from the world or someone else in the world.

We are the first examples to our children and as a matter of fact their first role models. They imitate everything they see us do. So if we teach our kids to be patient but we cannot show patience to them through our actions, then they tend to copy the same act and replay it to us. As parent we get frustrated because to us that is not what we are teaching them but that is also what they saw.

Sometimes we may be doing the right things but it is hard for our children to emulate, still don't give up. Discipline where necessary and continue to talk about it until the child begins to accept it deeply and show willingness to change.

You also have to check your child's surroundings to know what the problem is- sometimes the child may be listening to other kids' words or learning/copying their actions which to them is good because they have not seen the other kid's mom or dad discipline them. As you see negative attitudes, cut the wrong bud immediately with the word of God before they grow.

As parents we have to do the good things or let our light shine before men and our children so that they would see the outcome of it and then their trust in God as we are teaching them will grow. This will also help them to obey and show respect to us as their parents.

In Ephesians 6:1-3 "Children, obey your parents in the Lord, for this is right. 'Honor your father and mother' (this is the first commandment with a promise), 'that it may go well with you and that you may live long in the land'"

But who is going to teach these children how to obey and honor; unless they see us do it to our own parents or to the elderly. They show their dependency to us and we intend take up the responsibility for them to see how much we love them. But on our path we disrespect our own parents/the elderly in front of them and then we turn around and ask them to honor us. Really!!!!

You reap what you sow; remember!!

Every time our children show dependency on us and we intend show dependency on God, It makes it easier for the child to learn and know how to depend on God. We become the mediators between the child and God so, whatever we do before God the child learns it and also imitates. As they see progress in our relationship; they see how God is responsible to us and this makes it easier for the child to show honor and respect to God through how they show honor and respect to us. Because remember if they cannot do it to us; they cannot do it God. If they disrespects us and fill that guilt attached to disobedience, then they will feel it when they disrespect God. Don't tell me that the child can be right with God without being right with the parent by disrespecting them. They cannot receive the blessings of God. Again don't tell me that you are mean to somebody but you love God. Seriously!!!!!

We teach our children to focus their minds on so much church activities and traditions that these activities sort of invisibly take up their time and they begin to invest their time in it more than their time with God. So they went to church but do they know God. They missed the presence of God whiles they were in class learning about him; their minds and joy were focused on the activities they were going to do for everyone to see. These activities are good yet they can be distracting and make us busy and miss the presence of God. It is good for our kids to pause and be still to wait on the Lord. This way their focus can be shifted back to God.

Sometimes, I wonder and worry that our children in the churches can be distracted how much more those children outside who are being exploited for fame and money. Do they even get time to know about their maker?

Some questions to answer to help you know more about your child

1. What makes your child feel loved?
2. Does your child like it when you share time with them? Why?

3. What do you teach your children about?
4. How do you and your child feel at home together?
5. How often do you discipline your children?
6. Do your children feel bad about the discipline you give them? and what is your reaction and solutions to them
7. What do they enjoy doing with you?
8. Do you know what the hardest thing in their life is now?
9. Have you ever celebrated your children's good abilities and progress before?
10. How much time do you spend with your children?

CHAPTER 3

COMMUNICATION

Everything that God created have a way to communicate one way or the other. The thunder makes noise and you know it is about to rain, the tree makes noise and you know whether the wind is strong or calm. The sun shines it light and we feel the heat or enjoy it etc. excuse me to say this but even in a house that have mutes they still find a way to communicate. Communication is a strong pillar that when neglected even the strongest foundation can easily be broken.

Speech is an everyday item we can't do without and communication is an important tool in the family and home. Without communication a house or even a community would be dulled and care and affection would be lost. A home without proper communication is full of chaos and misunderstandings becomes the order of the day

A house that does not have a right communication system does not stand firm or is easily out of unity because the relationship amongst members are not right to begin with.

If you don't communicate with your children, you can't build a proper relationship with them. Likewise if you don't help them to have a proper communication with God they can't have a proper relationship with him. If your only system of communication is on phone, you and your children become strangers to each other when you meet at home. Whenever you are together their reactions toward you become awkward and they prefer staying in their rooms or at a friend's place or in school than to be around you.

In the same way, when, all the child know is how to pray and not how to communicate to God through his word, God becomes a stranger to him/her when he approaches the child, thus in church, the child prefer to stay on phone or play a game or chat with another friend instead of having his focus on God. The child only talks with God when he/she is in need because that is what they see you do every time.

I always tell my kids- if something is bothering you and you don't open your mouth to talk it out, nobody will know it and even offer help to you and then you cannot blame anybody either for that misfortune.

God knows our needs yet he told us to ask him through prayer, he did not say someone should be the only one to pray for us in church, but as individuals he asked us to pray to him so that we can build a relationship with him. But this kind of talk has to be in line with God's will. So if the child does not know his word how does the child know his will.

E.g. Somebody is bothering this child, and then the child starts to pray to God to kill this somebody or do something bad to this somebody so that the child will feel a certain satisfaction in the pain this somebody gets. God will not listen to this kind of prayer because he said: love your enemies and do good to those who hurt you, pray for those who accuse you. If this child doesn't get the response they want, they will grab a gun and kill this somebody themselves. Thus the child's heart is already filled with hate.

So in this case if we teach the child the will of God, the child will know that God also said if anyone lacks wisdom let him ask the Lord…

You and the child will pray about it for God's direction and pray for a change to happen in the other child's or this somebody who is bothering him or hers life. You help your child to stop doing things that calls for this somebody's attention and then reports it to the proper authorities.

As a parent, you need to have an active role in the child's spiritual development to help the child avoid severe struggles in his/her life ahead in the future.

Because there is proper communication system taught, the child when faced with challenges in life;

- Knows who to contact and talk to knowing that the grace of God is sufficient enough for them through that struggle
- The child find the peace in the truth that is in the word and are able to be calm knowing that he has the Lord on his side
- The child feels the freedom in depending on God and knows how to wait for their turn.

The communication between Jesus and Martha worked well that in John 11:21-23

²¹ Martha then said to Jesus: "Lord, if you had been here, my brother would not have died.²² yet even now I know that whatever you ask God for, God will give you." ²³ Jesus said to her: "Your brother will rise.

Meaning- she indeed chose what was right by changing her mind. I like this about her; she wasn't offended about Jesus' open corrections in front of her sister but instead trusted Jesus more with her whole self. Also I do not find any hate in her heart towards her sister.

As parents we should learn from Christ, who knew how to solve problems without creating offense for the other. Sometimes in correcting our children we tend to let the other person feel like they are the bad ones and the other won. But we should be able to show both of them the truth to maintain the love between them.

Some questions to help you build your relationship through communication

1. In your opinion, to what level do you agree that you are capable of dealing with your child's emotions appropriately?
2. How often do you help your child engage in activities which are educational outside the home and church?
3. How often do you have conversations with your child about what his/her problems are?
4. How well do you know your child?
5. How confident are you in your ability to support your child's learning good morals through life's challenges?

CHAPTER 4

VALUES AND INTEGRITY

As a parent you know that what defines you are the things in your heart and mind because these are the things that you control, and only you can allow people in; and also remember that adult behavior is learned as a child. So we ought to let the children know that materialism, where they come from, backgrounds etc. do not define them but the hidden things in their mind and hearts that are put into actions whether good or bad make others like or dislike them.

In this our modern day and time, integrity has been made to take the back seat and dishonesty and foolish gains have been made and allowed to champion our course of lives. We as parents have become so conceited that our way of life have been imparted into our children without realizing it. We have stopped practicing honesty, truthfulness, godliness, justices, and the likes in front of our children. Our children usually see us giving nasty and unpleasant replies to something or someone we disliked and they copied it without the parent realizing it. consequences for our actions whether good or bad have been turned into fun and entertainments so now the children believe they are right in anything they do and nobody can tell them what to do. We have chased our values out from our hearts and allowed money to rule. We have intertwined our fake values with materialism to the point that now a child thinks that because of the wealthy background he has, they can boss everyone around and do whatever they like without being punished for their actions. In so doing they even disrespect their elderly and seriously look down on others. Certain parents even disrespect themselves in front of their kids, how and what do you want these children to learn?

We do not show through examples to our children like standing tall and boasting about the truth you just told or the help you just gave to someone, instead, we show off the number of cars we have or the amount of money or girlfriends that we have. Some even smoke or drink in front of their kids. The child also copies what they see when they see you doing it freely without consequences. Our children express themselves through their actions and since we cannot control their behavior before they act, we have to use those moments as opportunities to teach them what is right and allow them to reflect on their wrong doings. Ask for your child's opinion in the matter and respect them. Too much work as a parent makes you neglect the future (your child) that you claim you are working for to make life comfortable. Children crave for love and attention so when they do not get these they develop a rebellious spirit to get the attention they wanted. If only you can cut down on your too much activities lifestyle then you can have enough time to fill and grow with your kids there by building better relationships with them and also becoming their confidants.

We pray that God should bless our children, remember that we get tested by the prayers we make and are we really sure we can pass these test in our current situations and lifestyles we have acquired as parents?

When we do not teach our children proper values, so many rebellious characters are formed and imparted into the child; their rebellious spirits take fear away; after all there is no one to rebuke them when they go wrong and they begin to disrespect adults or the elderly because whatever negative things they have been imparted with make friends with their souls and dictate to the child's mind and their character become influenced.

- Respect is also a value

Bible tells us that we are all born with an inborn sense of God's reality and a hint of what it is he wants from us.

Ecclesiastes 3:11

" He has made everything beautiful in its time. He has also set eternity in the human heart; yet no one can fathom what God has done from beginning to end.

When we as parents give respect to our children they reciprocate the action and through this it becomes easier to teach them to give respect to God. This right way of teaching and living not only help the child but also improve the quality of the child's social life whereby he is able to live peaceably with others. But if the child is not prepared well for these grounds, they tend to be self-centered, hurt others and don't really care about their actions. Life becomes difficult because they do not know their right from their left. Worst of all, they disregard the word of God and do whatever they want without a care or their conscience pricking them. Bible said: do unto others as you want them to do unto you. Luke 6: 31

Knowing this help them to be able to have proper respect for God through the relationship the build with God.

- Holding family meetings can also be a value- here, the purpose is to teach, discuss and work together to address difficult issues and then solve problems. Usually this kind of meeting help resolve or prevent strong emotional issues concerning especially the kids. We are able to help the child learn to forgive themselves and others as well.

Some questions to help you build your values

1. On average, how well does your child work independently on learning activities at home?
2. How motivated is your child to learn the topics covered in at home and in church?
3. How motivated are they to showcase their values, abilities and skills out there?
4. Do they stand by their beliefs or do they compromise easily?
5. Some people pursue some of their goals for a long time, and others change their goals frequently. Over the next several years, how likely is your child to continue to pursue one of his/her current goals or continue with family traditions?

CHAPTER 5

DEMONSTRATION THROUGH ACTIONS

What our children see both in and out of the home, they are more likely to do the same. Sometimes it gets difficult laying the godly foundations in our children because what they see outside the home may be stronger and overshadows what they see in the house. In this wise, the characters outside the home invisibly impart their characteristics in them thereby programming and conditioning their mindsets. They are able to remember these negative things quicker than the morals you teach at home.

If the children do not see their parents studying the word of God with them, praying with them, and respecting and obeying God's standards and principles they would prefer what is outside and ungodly to what is inside and godly. When we lay strong foundations and good principles based on God's word, we teach our children to learn a way of life and how to live it.

Once my son told me mommy you told me to have patience but why are you getting frustrated and impatient, suddenly, my heart skipped a beat and I realized how much my son was watching and learning. I made up my mind to do exactly what I teach.

You would be surprised how much our children have learned from us that they have not even showed to us, both good and bad. But only if the good were more than the bad then that would be a blessing. To our children how we react in times of situations help them to learn practically and fast. It also helps them to understand what we teach them. It also serves as a reference for them when they also find themselves in similar situations. Our children learn about responsibilities through us by watching how we take up our own responsibilities to bring about results. In order to lay these good foundations we have to allow and encourage our children to ask questions and give them problems to solve every now and then. Don't scare the children when they make mistakes but use their mistakes as opportunities to teach them about God and his love for them. Encourage the children to grow out of the mess they create instead of being scared to come out and staying in their mess. Let them know that God always want us to come out and grow to be matured in him so that he can give us matured stuff to handle for him. We will always be considered babies if we cannot grow out of our mess and no baby takes up hard tasks. We are able to enjoy the benefits and blessings of God in Christianity when we grow in God's word and mature in his spirit.

When we face trials and hard circumstances in our lives as parents, our first reaction sticks in the minds of our children. If we make it seem so easy by taking the easy way out or by way of cheating our way out of the process, then that is what they will learn and will do the same. But when we take up the challenge of walking through patiently, taking every step one at a time until we succeed and not give up our children will also learn this way of life to become better and matured people who can vision ahead even when they are in challenges. Our children will learn that they would also have trails and rough circumstances but they can overcome it. We should bring to their attention as early as possible that being Christians doesn't mean that they will not face challenges but that is how it brings them to the obedience of God. We teach them that through our sufferings God is made strong in our weakness.

As the children grow, they encounter opportunities or critical moments in their lives don't ignore them, turn and grow with them in those moments otherwise, you will lose them. Don't spiritualize everything, face their physical troubles with them and solve them physically and face the spiritual matters spiritually. This also help them to discipline themselves by setting or putting their lives in order. It helps them to distinguish physical things from the spiritual enabling them to tackle situations with the right tools and with the right mindset. They would also learn that God uses our circumstances as a process to build us so that we can be right with God inwardly to appear outwardly for others to see and emulates and this helps us to have the peace of God and stay out of trouble because they are guided by God's word. E.g. certain parents would want to show off by building castles for their children but after this what character would they use in maintaining it? Ask yourself. As parents we should remember that what we impart in our children are more important than what we build for them. Teaching them the right way to build that castle is much better than building it for them while they are busy doing their own thing and then asking them to keep it. It came easily to them so they will lose it easily too. when we don't teach our children the right way of living, they would always come back to their beginning and struggle to build their foundation whereas if they had learnt to build a good foundation of right living it would have been easier for them to keep building a solid one, and instead of destroying it they would rather keep building on it.

1. Do you practice respect in front of your children?
2. Do you do what you say or you just talk in front of your children

3. How do we solve problems?
4. What good character do you see in your child and you want to encourage him or her? Hard work, kindness, generosity, independence, etc.
5. What bad character de you see in your child and you want to discourage it?

CHAPTER 6

TEACHING ABOUT LIFE'S CHOICES

Each and every one of us including our children did not choose how, who or even where to be born but in the end we all have to learn to deal with it. As a wise way, we have to teach our children to be confident in themselves and not try to be someone else. What if you were born a king and you decided to be the servant you won't be able to handle the task well; you would always feel like you are being looked down upon and that you have more to give. Also what if you were born the servant and you decided to be the king you will be overwhelmed with the task and lose focus and your mind in the end. If everybody were the doctor who would be the nurse? And if everybody were the king, where would the people and the nation to rule be?

So strategically, God has designed each one of us to fill a certain purpose on earth. We all cannot fit in someone else's shoes, it would be too tight or too loose to walk in. We have to help them to figure themselves out and help them position themselves in their right opportunities. In life's choices, all of us including our children should know that certain prayers are not answered by God for good reasons best known in his word. Just like how we as parent would not give our children something that would harm them it is the same with God too. He gives you the best and you will not find sorrow attached to it unless we misuse his gift to us. We have to teach them that even though we do not get what we prayed for we still have to continue trusting and having faith in God for his perfect timing.

Jeremiah 29:11
" For I know the plans I have for you," declares the LORD, "plans to prosper you and not to harm you, plans to give you hope and a future.

We should teach our children:

- The Lord is the provider of our needs

Therefore, do not be anxious, saying, 'What shall we eat?' or 'What shall we drink?' or 'What shall we wear?' For the Gentiles seek after all these things, and your heavenly Father knows that you need them all. But seek first the kingdom of God and his righteousness, and all these things will be added to you. (Matthew 6:31-33)

Philippians 4:12-13 (NIV)
"I know what it is to be in need, and I know what it is to have plenty. I have learned the secret of being content in any and every situation, whether well fed or hungry, whether living in plenty or in want. I can do all this through him who gives me strength."

- He is always with us and he will not leave us nor forsake us

But the Helper, the Holy Spirit, whom the Father will send in my name, he will teach you all things and bring to your remembrance all that I have said to you. (John 14:26)

Deuteronomy 31:6 (NIV)
"Be strong and courageous. Do not be afraid or terrified because of them, for the Lord your God goes with you; he will never leave you nor forsake you."

- When we are tempted the Lord will provide a way out

No temptation has overtaken you that is not common to man. God is faithful, and he will not let you be tempted beyond your ability, but with the temptation he will also provide the way of escape, that you may be able to endure it. (1 Corinthians 10:13)

Psalm 46:1-3 (NIV)
"God is our refuge and strength, an ever-present help in trouble. Therefore we will not fear, though the earth give way and the mountains fall into the heart of the sea, though its waters roar and foam and the mountains quake with their surging."

- Our children should also learn from us that every actions they take or every choice they make have consequences attached to them and it would be better to rather choose to learn the good morals and values instead. E.g. honoring our parents, respect, and honesty. As parents we should also celebrate our children when they are able to meet these standards as way of encouragement to them to never be ashamed of practicing what is right because it is the narrow way that leads to no trouble but inner peace from God. On regular basis our children are faced with many challenges and they react with such impulse that it takes effort and practical knowledge to do the right thing so this form of celebration is a way of encouragement that builds and helps them to be confident in any situation to do the right thing so that they can also be proud of themselves.

- We should also teach our children about the choice of time wasting: if we don't put effort into something, we will not gain anything. If we don't take the risk of being bothered or provoked by the course, goals or visions we set for our lives we will never achieve anything. Every time we try to get up to achieve these we will face opposition from others-family members, enemies, friends, our own selves, etc. but we have to get up and keep going for the joy of the prize. There is always a hidden joy of contentment on a success achieved by one's self. All these oppositions will train you to be tough to sail through the hard storm and you can easily place value on what you have. If you compromise to the needs of those hurting you then you will be their puppet all your life and will never know what happiness and freedom is.

- people will define them based on what they need from them:

Another choice as parents we should look out for, for our children is that we should make them aware on how to look for opportunities and possibilities through the definition of others about them. Why?

Because sometimes a child is able to find who he/she is through the circumstances created by others.

Let say your child is a thinker, if there is no available situation what is there for the child to think about and create a solution for the problem. So sometimes the need others create for us would define us and push us to be who we are and where we ought to be. Somebody like young David in the bible, before he became a king, he had to go through a situation that had been created for his people to deal with. Here we realized that there was a need for his people- they needed a champion to fight for them and this created a cause for David. He saw a purpose through the people and the situation and because of that made a decision and became a champion for the people. He realized he was a warrior and throughout his kingship, he fought a lot and was always victorious.

Sometimes the situation others create for us would help us identify who we are.

- Another choice is to teach them to watch their attitude:

As parent if we want to discourage them from wallowing in their defeats of life then we should first let them see us showing restraint from self-blame, boxing ourselves down all the time, too much sadness in a situation etc. and rise up with wisdom to find solutions to the problem and not giving up until all possibilities have been exhausted. Sometimes we have to create fun and ask them for their opinion and also depending on the problem involve them if possible so that they can have ideas about problem solving. This improve their attitudes in problem solving for the future. It also helps our children know what to apply from their experiences and resources available to get or create the solutions needed especially at their work places and home.

CHAPTER 7

YOUR CHARACTER BRANDS YOU NOT WHAT YOU WEAR

Your character defines you; would you rather be called good or evil all the days of your life? Let us pause and consider who we are. How do people see us? Who do we think we are? Reason it out for yourself and weigh yourself on the good and evil scale. Well I am going to write about some hard truths about how we raise our kids and how some families are in our society.

A bad or wicked person is like a poisonous venom wherever he/she finds himself or herself grief is caused to others. Their influence on others are deadly.

These people quietly makes evil plans and causes trouble; they tempt people and draw them away from taking the right path. Their thoughts and plans are evil and they wants evil things and they also makes evil plans which destroy others. This is why their desires are worth nothing. Because they want wicked things they would fail totally. Their words destroys their neighbors and everyone suffers because of them. When they are not around people shout for joy and feel they are free but when they are around they feel oppressed but because they are foolish, they do not consider this yet they keep on being cruel and will bring troubles upon themselves. They provide necessary means to carry out the sins they want to commit without a care in the conscience.

Good character is shown in how we react in any given situation. Actions speaks louder than words and so in the end you are judged based on what you showed outside.

Proverbs 28:6 – "Better is a poor man who walks in his integrity than a rich man who is crooked in his ways."

God knows our intentions so we need to watch out and have change of mind in our dealings.

Some people don't care what they use their bodies for, forgetting that their bodies are the temple of God and that anyone who destroys it He would also destroy them. We also have to watch the kind of company we associate ourselves with because they can corrupt our character. A person who watch his or her character carefully is called blessed.

Let us look at these verses below to describe and tell us if we are good or bad in the sight of God.

Psalm 1:1 Blessed is the one who does not walk in step with the wicked or stand in the way that sinners take or sit in the company of mockers, but whose delight is in the law of the LORD, and who meditates on his law day and night. That person is like a tree planted by streams of water, which yields its fruit in season and whose leaf does not wither— whatever they do prospers. Not so the wicked! They are like chaff that the wind blows away.

Proverbs 22:24-25 Do not make friends with a hot-tempered person, do not associate with one easily angered, or you may learn their ways and get yourself ensnared.

1 John 2:15-17
Do not love the world or anything in the world. If anyone loves the world, love for the Father is not in them. For everything in the world—the lust of the flesh, the lust of the eyes, and the pride of life—comes not from the Father but from the world. The world and its desires pass away, but whoever does the will of God lives forever

Proverbs 14:7 Stay away from a fool, for you will not find knowledge on their lips.

Matthew 5:30 And if your right hand causes you to stumble, cut it off and throw it away. It is better for you to lose one part of your body than for your whole body to go into hell.

Here I would say that it would be better to lose your friends, money, pride, fame, materialism or something you consider valuable and go to Heaven that to have them and go to hell.

1 Corinthians 5:11-13
But now I am writing to you that you must not associate with anyone who claims to be a brother or sister but is sexually immoral or greedy, an idolater or slanderer, a drunkard or swindler. Do not even eat with such people.

What business is it of mine to judge those outside the church? Are you not to judge those inside?

God will judge those outside. "Expel the wicked person from among you."

Proverbs 6:16-19
There are six things that the Lord hates, seven that are an abomination to him: haughty eyes, a lying tongue, and hands that shed innocent blood, a heart that devises wicked plans, feet that make haste to run to evil, a false witness who breathes out lies, and one who sows discord among brothers.

Are these verses speaking to you? Do you know where you belong?

Are you coming up with solutions to fix the problems yet?

1.   John 6:67-71

So Jesus said to the twelve, "Do you want to go away as well?" [68] Simon Peter answered him, "Lord, to whom shall we go? You have the words of eternal life, and we have believed, and have come to know, that you are the Holy One of God." Jesus answered them, "Did I not choose you, the twelve? And yet one of you is a devil." He spoke of Judas the son of Simon Iscariot, for he, one of the twelve, was going to betray him.

2. Ecclesiastes 7:1 A good name is better than precious ointment, and the day of death than the day of birth.

3. Galatians 5:22-23

But the fruit of the Spirit is love, joy, peace, patience, kindness, goodness, faithfulness, [23] gentleness, self-control; against such things there is no law.

4. Matthew 7:17

So, every healthy tree bears good fruit, but the diseased tree bears bad fruit.

5. Romans 5:3-5

Not only that, but we rejoice in our sufferings, knowing that suffering produces endurance, and endurance produces character, and character produces hope, and hope does not put us to shame, because God's love has been poured into our hearts through the Holy Spirit who has been given to us.

CHAPTER 8

MATURATION- EMBRACING OUR IMPERFECTIONS

God is perfect but man is not because we sin always and need the spirit of God to live in to guide and teach us. We cannot make ourselves perfect until Christ comes in. so the bible said:

Proverbs 3:5-6 New International Version (NIV)
⁵ Trust in the Lord with all your heart and lean not on your own understanding; ⁶ in all your ways submit to him, and he will make your paths straight.[a]

James 3:2
For we all stumble in many ways if anyone does not stumble in what he says, he is a perfect man, able to lead the whole body as well

Philippians 3:12
Not that I have already obtained it or have already become perfect, but I press on so that I may lay hold of that for which also I was laid hold of by Christ Jesus

1 Corinthians 13:10
But when the perfect comes, the partial will be done away.

We all know that God created us in his own image and after his likeness, but when man sinned we retained the image of God but his likeness was taken away and so we look like God but our character is not like God anymore. But God did not leave us there; in that whiles we were yet sinners Christ died for us. Because God loved us so much, he gave his only son to die for us so that whoever believes in him should not perish but have everlasting life. Initially, man was perfect so God gave the responsibility of naming everything he created to man and whatever man called it, so it was. But now that we are not perfect, God said, if any of us lacks wisdom then we should ask him who give it generously without measure but the condition is that we have to believe that we have receive it.

So as parent or children everything that we want to accomplish in this life of ours we have to commit to God so that he will direct our path for us.

- We think and say lots of things to accomplish yet, we stumble and find ourselves wanting, and that makes us imperfect. So we need the strength of Christ to do all things so that all glory can go back to him.
- We feel pain and distress and that makes us imperfect so we have to call to on God to help through and comfort us.
- Sometimes we think we are standing but we may have fallen, we sin easily and that makes us imperfect so we need Christ in lives to help us overcome sin and put on us his garment of righteousness to overcome sin.
- We are tested to find obedience in us yet we fall and show disobedience that makes us imperfect therefore we need Christ and his spirit to dwell in us to help us obey God.

If we are able to keep the word of God in us then the love of God is perfected and then we know that we are in him.

If we love God then all things would work together for good, for those we are called according to his purpose.

Because we are imperfect and working towards God's perfection through Christ, he has laid down character for us to build to make our walk in this world shine present his glory. He wants want us to fruitful in:

➢ Love- God, neighbor, ourselves, enemies
➢ Joy- be happy in times of trouble and good occasions trusting in him always
➢ Peace- in troubled times and happy times let the peace of God reign

- Patience- every time we rush in life, we always come back to re-start so God wants us to patient at all times and in everything we do.
- Kindness- be kind to everyone you may be doing it to angels
- Goodness- be good to everyone
- Faithfulness- be faithful to God in all things both small and big
- Gentleness- Jesus said we should learn from him because he is humble and gentle in the heart.
- Self-control- in all things we should exercise self-control.

1 Corinthians 10:23 says:
"I have the right to do anything," you say—but not everything is beneficial. "I have the right to do anything"—but not everything is productive.

We also have to strife to think and do whatever is:

- ➢ True
- ➢ Honorable
- ➢ Just
- ➢ Pure
- ➢ Lovely
- ➢ Commendable
- ➢ Excellence
- ➢ And anything that is worthy of praise

CHAPTER 9

THE HURT IN LOVE/ PERSONALITY FACTORS

A. Certain parents have neglected their own children because of a certain pain the children may have caused in their hearts. Sometimes the parents don't even want to hear the names of these children mentioned even in the home or to their hearing. They would not accept even their apologies or gifts. The claim of the parent is that this is the child they loved the most and spent so much on and they had high expectation for them. But usually, this claim is not even love but an obsession they developed towards these children. When the children grow to certain ages and they can't take it anymore they decide to rebel in way to free themselves. Some also just want their parents to trust them enough to allow them to explore life and to better understand the lessons their parents taught them. But the obsession on the parent's part block all arguments and the parent begin to develop hatred in their hearts towards the children. Sometimes, certain children for no reason just rebel against the good advice that their parents give to them. But as parents no matter what we must still leave some room for them for repentance. Sometimes when we neglect these children, they develop low self-esteem, they feel less and less accepted in life, it may show as though they are happy outwardly but inwardly they struggle a lot with less or no peace in their lives.

Romans 15:7 says: Accept one another, then, just as Christ accepted you, in order to bring praise to God.

As parents, when we do not accept our children the way they are and reconcile with them when they repent or change their minds and attitudes but then we decide to break them over differences of opinion and lifestyles, we leave a huge gap for judgement upon them for which they will carry that heavy cross until we help them unload it and take a breath. We are so quick to judge them but we forget that sometimes we are/may be their cause or source of problems. Growing and maturing from their mistakes also become a problem because they have not been able to cross over that huge gap created.

Oftentimes when we maltreat our children's feelings and distance them from us, we often tell ourselves it is their faults and that they are not important to us but when we look carefully we realize that we are lying, because we also don't feel the peace we want within ourselves and we struggle the most trying to prove to them that we are always right. But we forget that every child needs the upper hand to lift them up from the dirt; as they are rising up they look up to see the face of the one who is helping them get back up and when they grab that hand to rise, they feel another strength transferred to them which keeps them balanced and stable. This contact invisibly intensify their relationship and improve upon their respect for each other and in so doing the children easily humble themselves by submitting to the person who offered the help they received. But if we leave them sitting down in their mess using a form of scare tactics to intimidate them and refuse to offer any form of help, what they see is the monster in us and the pressure to stay where they are. They get scared to approach us for a reconciliation and so we only leave them the choice of rebelling in their heart towards us. Remember if this attitude keeps going on between the two when either of you pray the Lord will not listen unless there is a reconciliation. But if the parent or the child has made an effort to reconcile and the other party refused, then that party is to be blamed for his or her non-answered prayers. Yet again, if the parent or the child is doing something abominable unto God, then they should know that God has first of all rejected them unless they repent and reconcile with Him otherwise they will have no peace in their lives.

Some Natural ways to release our anger for everyone who may be reading this book. We all get angry but keeping anger in your heart will make you unhealthy or may control you to do something that may cost you dearly. So these are some natural therapy I developed in writing to help anyone through such times.

Ephesians 4:26-27
Be angry and do not sin; do not let the sun go down on your anger, and give no opportunity to the devil

Ephesians 4:31
Let all bitterness and wrath and anger and clamor and slander be put away from you, along with all malice.

Proverbs 19:11
Good sense makes one slow to anger, and it is his glory to overlook an offense.

B. Natural ways to release your anger that I came up with along the journey of life:

This is an inspiration that I would like to share with everyone who gets the opportunity to read this book. It's been on my heart to share this for a while now and I think I have finally gotten the chance. This is about ways and directions to release your anger and relieve yourself from the stress it brings about. As we are all journeying through this life, I have realized one common thing that almost everyone share, and that is everyone get angry one way or the other. But then the aftermath of how we used our anger and the decisions we make counts the most. Anger is an emotion which can be either good or bad, at least it helps you know that you are not dead. It helps others to know their limit to you and how much they can control you. It also helps to communicate what is in the mind to others. Anger can bring about something positive so it can also bring about something negative. On the part of the negative it invokes resentment coming from the heart and the aftermath of it mostly can be deadly. The negative part is what I am going to discuss with you. We are going to find some natural ways to release our anger and yet still make the right decisions without regretting them.

We get angry easily but letting go becomes a problem. The very things or people we want to find joy in usually are the people who anger us the most; our family, colleagues, friends, in relationships or even some material things that we possess etc. in our anguish through anger we often feel pain and unanswered questions. Who is responsible and how would the problem be solved are but a few things we think about.

A few natural ways I would be sharing with you as a way of releasing your anger and stress are:

1. Be mad with yourself; relieve your stress

Psalm 4:4
Be angry, and do not sin; ponder in your own hearts on your beds, and be silent.

As you are assuming that it is the entire fault of the offender think again you may have missed some details on your part. And also yes it may have been the entire fault of the offender. But why are you the only one struggling this much and also why are you not willing to let it go; trying so hard to earn pity from others. Here is a chance for you to vent or release the anger that has built up in you for a while now. Instead of punching a perishable thing that will re-cost you money later on or hurling insults at the person and later on regretting it or yet still getting so mad with yourself and getting into a habit which will cost you and prevent you from getting yourself back in later years, why don't you do this instead.

a. Get an empty room where you can be alone, your room or car would be enough. Or get an empty space, an empty park or your back yard would be enough. The point is for you to be alone without any disturbances.

b. Get two chairs one for you and one for the other person or the offender. As you sit on the other one imagine/assume your opponent is sitting on the other one. Or when you are at the park or backyard assume the other person is there too.

c. Look directly at the chair or the side where you think the other person would be. You are doing this because in this space no one would see you or be able to criticize you. You have the chance to access the problem all over again with much calm and have nobody confronting you or arguing with you.

Ecclesiastes 10:4 If the ruler's temper rises against you, do not abandon your position, because composure calms great offenses

Proverbs 24:29
Do not say, "I will do to him as he has done to me; I will pay the man back for what he has done."

d. Start laying out the problems one by one without missing a point because you are at liberty to do so at this point. Here you are carefully allowed to criticize the person, but don't forget to admit to where you were wrong too. If you would want to write them down too that is ok. Mark out your wrongs with red ink or a color of your choice. Now with the same scale you are using to accuse the other use the same on yourself; be fair about it

Deuteronomy 25:13-16
"You shall not have in your bag two kinds of weights, a large and a small. You shall not have in your house two kinds of measures, a large and a small. A full and fair weight you shall have, a full and fair measure you shall have, that your days may be long in the land that the LORD your God is giving you. For all who do such things, all who act dishonestly, are an abomination to the LORD your God.

Ephesians 4:26 BE ANGRY, AND yet DO NOT SIN; do not let the sun go down on your anger,

e. As you are doing this with no interruptions, at some point you would realize that you were also at fault too. Unless it was actually the entire fault of the other person. Be humble about it. Don't be happy that it was not your fault and rejoice at the other person's fault as though you were waiting for that to happen. You will give the devil a foothold if you do that.

James 4:7 Submit yourselves therefore to God. Resist the devil, and he will flee from you.

2. Be calm with yourself

After you are through with the first step, try to be calm with yourself. It not as easy as it sounds, but it is one of the best solutions to start with. In doing this, you will be helping yourself analyze the whole situation and to know where the problem started from. Why there is this sort of problem and how many people are involved. And also how to go about solving it. With reference to carefully criticizing the invisible person remember to admit your faults too. This way there would be a fair play here and making decisions become less hard on you. Being calm also relaxes your body and mind allowing you an ease of understanding to digest every action and consequences from the decisions you would make.

Proverbs 29:11
A fool gives full vent to his spirit, but a wise man quietly holds it back.

Proverbs 25:28
A man without self-control is like a city broken into and left without walls.

3. Draw out the problems and think of solutions

In your calm state, start drawing out the real problem and the reason why this problem came about. Though we may not always have the answers to the problems yet knowing the problem and what is causing it is good.

At least you can research on how to solve it.

Also knowing the solution is the best since you can also help resolve the problem with much ease. Because by presenting your opinions, you would have thought of and considered the other person's emotions and understanding of things or issues.

Colossians 3:8
But now you must put them all away: anger, wrath, malice, slander, and obscene talk from your mouth

James 1:5 says If any of you lacks wisdom, let him ask God, who gives generously to all without reproach, and it will be given him. .

4. Talk it out

Philippians 4:13 I can do all things through Christ who strengthens me.

This step takes courage because

a. You would be admitting your fault too if you are indeed at fault
b. You would be feeling like the other person has won or have the upper hand and you are submitting

c. You may even feel like your pride have been hurt

But let me ask you; 'what is your pride if you are dying slowly from the stress or distance you have created for yourself. What more is your pride if you are losing more than you are gaining?'

Wouldn't it be better if you could talk things out and have a clear conscience, peaceful mind and heart and being full of happiness and stress-free than to suffer silently while bottling up much anger and more unsolved problems.

Talking things out is one of the best solutions you can ever come across.

a. Take courage to approach the other person- this way you hold much power to direct the course of the discussion and you determine how much emotions to draw from the other person. On the other hand if you are approached, be on your best behavior or temperament giving ears to the discussion at hand. You still hold power with your emotions and good manners between you and the other party. But if you cannot control your emotions and the other party can, then there would be a switch in power and the other party now gets the opportunity to lead the discussion which may or may not end well to the expected end you envisioned.

Philippians 2:14-16
Do everything without grumbling or arguing, so that you may become blameless and pure, "children of God

without fault in a warped and crooked generation." Then you will shine among them like stars in the sky as you hold firmly to the word of life.

b. Be first to apologize – this way you give a responsibility to the other person. Doing this doesn't reduce your pride or make you less human but rather increase your chance of freedom from stress and from unnecessary hard feelings. When you do your part the rest lies with the other person and you would know you are free. Being forgiven is sweet but forgiving someone is even sweeter.

Proverbs 20:24 "A person's steps are directed by the Lord. How then can anyone understand their own way?"

Philippians 2:2-8

Complete my joy by being of the same mind, having the same love, being in full accord and of one mind. Do nothing from rivalry or conceit, but in humility count others more significant than yourselves. Let each of you look not only to his own interests, but also to the interests of others. Have this mind among yourselves, which is yours in Christ Jesus, who, though he was in the form of God, did not count equality with God a thing to be grasped....

c. Talk about the problem- don't leave the problems hanging without discussing it this way each of you will analyze and know how, where, why and who is causing the problem and how the problem came about. This also gives room to make up with each other through sharing and discussing concerned issues. This is when each of you have accepted your faults and old wounds begin to heal and also distances created patches up, a new joy sort of fill your heart and you fill like a heavy burden have been lifted off your shoulders. Note- make sure you accept your fault amicably.

Philippians 4:4-7 "Rejoice in the Lord always. I will say it again: Rejoice! Let your gentleness be evident to all. The Lord is near. Do not be anxious about anything, but in every situation, by prayer and petition, with thanksgiving, present your requests to God. And the peace of God, which transcends all understanding, will guard your hearts and your minds in Christ Jesus.

Ephesians 4:25

Therefore, having put away falsehood, let each one of you speak the truth with his neighbor, for we are members one of another.

d. Bring out your solutions- sharing your opinions would lead to the best solutions that best solves the problem. In talking it out, use soft answers, mild expressions, deliver your words with kindness and tenderness showing humility and submission and this as I believe and you will believe it too will work upon the passion of the other, weakening his/her resentment and break and scatter the storm formed in the chest. But in the opposite way when you use severe or grievous words it will stir up more anger. Don't be rough or scornful, proud and haughty and also overbearing to be handled.

Colossians 4:5-6 Be wise in the way you act toward outsiders; make the most of every opportunity. Let your conversation be always full of grace, seasoned with salt, so that you may know how to answer everyone."

Proverbs 15:1
A soft answer turns away wrath but a harsh word stirs up anger.

Proverbs 15:23
A person finds joy in giving an appropriate reply—and how good is a timely word!

So in conclusion don't try to bottle up your anger and be sick release them and be free and have power, love and sound mind.

Colossians 3:12-14

Put on then, as God's chosen ones, holy and beloved, compassionate hearts, kindness, humility, meekness, and patience, bearing with one another and, if one has a complaint against another, forgiving each other; as the Lord has forgiven you, so you also must forgive. And above all these put on love, which binds everything together in perfect harmony

CHAPTER 10

MY HOME

Do you feel like running away from home or is your home the best place you could ever be? Are you afraid to face your feelings because you are scared it will cause friction between you and your family? Are you criticized for every little thing you do at home? Then let us work it out together and find the solutions we seek.

Often times we love to be in other people's homes because we feel loved or secured, happy and full of laughter. Other times we feel like we can do whatever we want in somebody's home and not ours. To us, all the people in our homes don't understand us. But don't forget you also don't understand them. You and the people you consider as your family have not worked hard to acknowledge and accept your feelings yet. Negative reactions to situations usually contributes to these unlikeable behaviors. Parents, sometimes our children crave our attention seriously, other times too some children are never held accountable for their actions, and they are left alone without proper discipline to do whatever they please. There are yet certain homes where the children sort of have too much power e.g. financial power, holds a high position in life and because of this they intimidate the other family members including their parents. Frustration easily gets you get mad at the slightest sayings you hear from them and every action from them irritates you. You storm out without any explanation and goes straight to where you think you can find comfort only to realize you still don't belong there but you are just a guest of theirs. This is because when it comes to important matters of that family and decision making you are seriously excluded and your opinion does not count. So what is driving you out of your own home; a place where you belong and no one can take your place. Why do you feel so unhappy with yourself? Sometimes, the very place we are abandoning can be our greatest opportunity that we seek for. The experience in having a little discomfort, disappointments and anxiety build us to face greater challenges in the future. Whereas if we avoid these we would keep facing them always until we overcome.

Could it be that you don't not find love, peace, good, trustworthiness, creativity in the place you call home or you are not humble, organized, compassionate and generous enough to receive or accept good instructions from those above and around you. Also do you feel low self-esteem because you are surrounded by people who are above your level of life or intelligence and give you the feel of being intimidated?

I urge you to change yourself first and make it worthy of living and the home will be affected someway somehow. Be completely humble and gentle; be patient, bearing with one another in love. Make every effort to keep the unity of the Spirit through the bond of peace. Learn to work in unity and in the knowledge of Jesus and be matured in the growth of the Holy Spirit and then you will no longer be tossed here and there like the waves of the sea and be blown by the cunning and craftiness of people and your own deceitful thoughts. If you learn to speak the truth and be respectful the home will become a pleasant place to be in.

We sometimes get ourselves so worried over so many unnecessary stuff that take our time and efforts. And we also like to complain a lot and most of the time it is about others and how they are being mean to us. We become so self-centered that we skip the others feeling and always think of how mean they are to us. If we should direct our attention a little bit to what they say we may find some truth that concerns us. instead of being selfish and unhappy, we should learn to use such opportunity into being productive, discipline and hard work to accomplish our goals. We are all praying to God to show us where our strengths and skills or talent lies in us. The good things or skills we cannot find in us easily, others may find it for us through these kind of interactions. It is our duty to discern to find what is ours through them even if they use the meanest way to do it. You would be surprised that at the end of the day they helped you build yourself for who you are now.

In your home what goals do you set for yourself and others – if you seek others well- being yours will be met as well. If you want happiness and joy you will get it because you will work hard to create it. but is it just for yourself; remember, as long as others are happy because of you, you will be happy too. If you treat the members of your home as if they were part of you, you will earn your respect from them but if you treat them as if they were something else you will also be unhappy.

Which area of your home and family, can you be a part of? identify it – be it education, charity, business, manufacturing, sales, investment, agriculture, ranching, entertainer etc. identify your position in your home and fulfill your part to make it a home. But in all these let God come first and guide you.

Sometimes the best thing you can do at home is to relax and be open minded, play some encouraging music or sleep while you can. Sometimes as you relax you begin to know more about yourself and how you can better be your best.

During your hour of rest it can help you spend quality time with family, friends or even yourself to experience the gift that life has to offer.

As you take time to rest the burden on your mind also lessens thus giving you less stress. Solutions to the problems may be staring at you at the corner of your home or in your mind smiling at you and asking; why it took you so long to find it earlier; I have been here all this while; it will say. Resting also helps you to stay out of trouble and allows you to enjoy your home. But you will find good rest in Christ Jesus. When you are anxious about something give the worries to him and try to rest. When we work too much we tend to be burdened and easily gets irritated and also we become vulnerable to disobey God and disappoint our families.

That is why God gave us a day to rest and to surrender to Him in trust. Spending quality time help build relationships and strengthen resolutions. We are part of the homes we create therefore sharing joyful moments very often prepare us for good health, and give us a sense of belongingness. The home including the family become a pillar and your source of strength so make your home good so that you can always go back to it.

CHAPTER 11

OUR FAMILY DESERT TIMES

This next chapter talks about our battles that we face during our lonely times as individuals whether you are old or young, parent or a child. But at the end of it all we seek growth and maturity. Throughout our struggles, I called it the dessert moments of our lives.

The desert is a dry, barren, very hot and cold and silent place. There are not flowing rivers or streams that run freely and when you find yourself on this path you really thirst for water and not have a drop for months. If the physical desert is so hostile, then how much more hostile the spiritual desert would be. There are evidence of physical things that makes one know that this is a desert like the sand, the heat and vast big sandy land with no trees or water. But in a spiritual desert what do you see nothing, except for the pain and anxiety you go through and the wish that they all go away immediately.

In this desert one can really feel very lonely and very much depressed, thus there are nobody there to go through it with you and feel what you feel. Even those who try to encourage you, only do so from the sympathy and the love they feel but no one really feel very anxious and desperate like you do. They only think about you for a while and forget about you in their sleep while you can't sleep at all.

Deserts are formed when something gets in the way of rain which brings freshness to life. So on the desert finding life worth things can be difficult because they can wither away as easily as they came. A big mountain could be blocking someone's awaited blessing from coming which leaves the person in despair and frustration.

In this desert it can feel like the Lord most High has really abandoned you and all the people who claim they would be there for you suddenly leave. We begin to struggle, doing everything we can to survive. Sometimes, we try to prove to ourselves and others that we can survive and the more we try, the more we stay in our struggle feeling very lost than when we first began. And then all we can do is to wallow in tears. This is when our eyes and heart are opened to see how others are succeeding and how we are losing all the time and then sometimes instead of surrendering to God we begin to feel very bitter in our heart and then start envying those around us and wishing them to be like us.

But remember, the desert is not all about that, sometimes it is our sins, yes, but sometimes it is for God's greater cause in our life. And so He allows us to meet the dangers and the hostile things on the desert to draw out our trust in him for He has said "fear not for I am with you"

Though we always want to walk on mountain tops as overcomers, the Lord sometimes makes us walk in the valley to show us how to climb the mountain to be overcomers not so we can stand and be proud of ourselves and say we did it but to show us how to be humble and acknowledge him as our God and father.

CHAPTER 12

KNOW YOUR SURROUNDINGS ON THE DESERT

Those who have traveled the physical desert would know that there are hostile things that can consume another life without mercy as it is a matter of life and death on a desert. It is not so different from spiritual desert. There are things we cannot see which keep pursuing us every time; and how can we overcome things that we cannot see.

Physically, if someone is holding a knife or gun at you, you panic, but and sometimes you can talk your way through to convince them but how can you convince someone you can't see?

But you know what the Lord said, "in all things give thanks to him"

Mark 1:9-13

9 One day Jesus came from Nazareth in Galilee, and John baptized him in the Jordan River. 10 As Jesus came up out of the water, he saw the heavens splitting apart and the Holy Spirit descending on him 1 like a dove. 11 And a voice from heaven said, "You are my dearly loved Son, and you bring me great joy." 12 At once the Spirit sent him out into the wilderness, 13 and he was in the wilderness forty days, being tempted[a] by Satan. He was with the wild animals, and angels attended him.

Jesus the son of God was driven into the desert to be tempted so we see that God allow us these opportunities in the desert for spiritual growth and dependence on Him.

Why? Because the Hidden need and the truth of our nature are revealed to us but if only we can see God in those times can we ever survive?

Jesus was tempted in three ways:

Luke 4:1-13
1 Then Jesus, full of the Holy Spirit, returned from the Jordan River. He was led by the Spirit in the wilderness, 2 where he was tempted by the devil for forty days. Jesus ate nothing all that time and became very hungry. 3 Then the devil said to him, "If you are the Son of God,

tell this stone to become a loaf of bread." 4 But Jesus told him, "No! The Scriptures say, 'People do not live by bread alone.' " 5 Then the devil took him up and revealed to him all the kingdoms of the world in a moment of time. 6 "I will give you the glory of these kingdoms and authority over them," the devil said, "Because they are mine to give to anyone I please. 7 I will give it all to you if you will worship me."

8 Jesus replied, "The Scriptures say, 'You must worship the LORD your God and serve only him.' "

9 Then the devil took him to Jerusalem, to the highest point of the Temple, and said, "If you are the Son of God, jump off! 10 For the Scriptures say, 'He will order his angels to protect and guard you.

11 And they will hold you up with their hands so you won't even hurt your foot on a stone.' "

12 Jesus responded, "The Scriptures also say, 'You must not test the LORD your God.'" 13 When the devil had finished tempting Jesus, he left him until the next opportunity came.

The necessities of life are usually what we are tempted with in our desert battles:

- Our daily bread- food, shelter, money, material needs etc. not that it is not good to have this things after all God said it is He who gives us the power to make wealth. But to make it our first priority in life is what we are talking about. It is said
Seek first the kingdom of God and his righteousness and all these things would be added to you.

- Power and control – though some are leaders and others are followers yet when power fall in their hands the desire in them rise so much that they will do anything to keep that power. To them controlling people and circumstances and things in their own life means much more to them than anything about their spiritual life. So before you take up power submit to God for it is He who set kings on the throne and dethrone them.
- Showing off by taking matters into our own hands without seeking the spiritual guidance of God. Sometimes we want to prove we are on top of things without giving God a chance in our difficulties and letting him prove who he is through us so others can depend on him. But instead we want others to depend on us and see us

as though it is we who are capable of anything and everything. But you know what God said " He resists the proud" therefore this is the time we need to be more humble in our thoughts and actions and let God lead the way through us.

CHAPTER 13

BE STILL

Be still for what God has intended in the inside of us is being tested to bring out the best in us and who we are in Christ and also to deepen our relationship with him.

There is no school on earth that has been built to teach us how to fight uncertainties in life and then award us a certificate showing that we have pass the test.

But you know what? When one accept Christ as their Lord and personal savior, the spirit of God lives in them and directs their paths so that in their desert times or trial times He works with them to build a strong character that depicts Christ's nature and a strong relationship that brings us closer and makes us depend on God with everything we've got.

People who have been in a warfare really don't jubilate when they become victorious but allow others to cheer for them because they know what they have been through and what it took for them to get that far and so they remain humble and keep waiting on God for directions.

Sometimes, it seems that God is not there; but it will be so when we are doing all the actions and trying to find solutions here and there. Just like the disciples in the boat; when the storm hit them they tried to find solutions on their own until they became calm and realized Jesus was in the boat. He was sleeping because they did not invite him in the trouble they were facing but when they finally called upon him, he spoke to the storm and suddenly everything became calm. Therefore let us be still and invite God in our storm for he is closer than we think. He is only waiting to be called upon. For He said, "call unto me in the days of trouble and I will answer you and show you great and mighty things.

CHAPTER 14

SURRENDER AND LOOK FOR POSSIBLE GROWTH

In the midst of our battles, there is nothing we can do about it but to surrender unto God. Queen Ester did so when her country men were in trouble. King David did so every time in his life to inquire of Lord before he made any move. Shedrach, Meshach, and Abednego did in the midst of fire, Daniel did in the lion's den, etc.

Through these battles we go through, we come to learn and grow in faith, trust, obedience, love and how to appreciate things of God.

One who has been desperate in his or her life learn to Trust God in times of trouble as well as depend on him.

In this times we desperately need faith to survive and so we begin to seek out God and his promises over our lives and begin to believe them and are also encouraged to pray more and expect more from God. Our dependency in obedience is what makes us humble and draw God towards us and this is when we begin to know who He is in our lives.

Through our battles, we learn to obey God's word through the bible, our pastor's counselling, and every word of encouragement we receive from others. And this words become our source of strength that walk with us every day. We also learn to let things go and not be bothered by them because we trust in God that He has dealt with our problems.

Romans 5:3-4
Not only that, but we rejoice in our sufferings, knowing that suffering produces endurance, and endurance produces character, and character produces hope,

Though the answers we seek might not come immediately as we need them, we learn how to endure through the hardship and allow God to stand by us through it all. We also learn the comfort of God which stays with us every minute in our lives reminding us of God's daily presence in our lives than the comfort of men which fades away easily.

1 Chronicles 16:11

Seek the LORD and his strength; seek his presence continually!

As the desert demands Obedience to it way of life, so we also learn Obedience through God's way of life. We develop instincts that help us differentiate good from evil in God's way. We learn to survive on what we have with God thus what God give us and tell us to do is what we are required to do without hesitation. We begin to feel the tangible love and presence of God in us which we cannot hide but share with everybody we come across.

Finally, we learn to submit our will and ways to God and He intends take charge and control it to bring us to the expected end.

CHAPTER 15

TRUST IN THE PROCESS OF GROWTH AND TAKE ACTION

2 Timothy 2:15 Study to show thyself approved unto God, a workman that needed not to be ashamed.

Be diligent in your journey study with God not to please men but to be approved by God. Not to receive favor or be praised by men but to receive divine approval. Be faithful in your duties so that when you look back you will not regret your deeds. But if you are doing this to be praised by men then you are not God's servant.

King David and Moses lived their lives in the desert, and God entrusted them with his people. With the skills God has taught them they led God's people to Him instead of seeking the praise of men. They withstood the test the people gave them and depended on God's direction. God's wants us to use the skills we acquire in the desert to lead others to him whiles depending on his every word and trusting in Him.

Ephesians 4:15
but speaking the truth in love, we are to grow up in all aspects into Him who is the head, even Christ

Colossians 1:10
so that you will walk in a manner worthy of the Lord, to please Him in all respects,

bearing fruit in every good work and increasing in the knowledge of God

1 Thessalonians 3:12
and may the Lord cause you to increase and abound in love for one another, and for all people, just as we also do for you;

Hebrews 6:1
Therefore leaving the elementary teaching about the Christ, let us press on to maturity, not laying again a foundation of repentance from dead works and of faith toward God,

2 Peter 1:5
Now for this very reason also, applying all diligence, in your faith supply moral excellence, and in your moral excellence, knowledge,

2 Peter 1:6
and in your knowledge, self-control, and in your self-control, perseverance, and in your perseverance, godliness,

2 Peter 3:18
but grow in the grace and knowledge of our Lord and Savior Jesus Christ To Him be the glory, both now and to the day of eternity. Amen.

Samuel 2:26
Now the boy Samuel was growing in stature and in favor both with the LORD and with men.

Luke 1:80
And the child continued to grow and to become strong in spirit, and he lived in the deserts until the day of his public appearance to Israel

Luke 2:52
And Jesus kept increasing in wisdom and stature, and in favor with God and men.

Acts 9:22
But Saul kept increasing in strength and confounding the Jews who lived at Damascus by proving that this Jesus is the Christ.

2 Thessalonians 1:3
We ought always to give thanks to God for you, brethren, as is only fitting, because your faith is greatly enlarged, and the love of each one of you toward one another grows ever greater

www.ingramcontent.com/pod-product-compliance
Lightning Source LLC
Chambersburg PA
CBHW030118100526
44591CB00009B/443